KNOW YOUR BODY

YOUR STOMACH

By George Fittleworth

Gareth Stevens
PUBLISHING

P9-BYY-914

Please visit our website, www.garethstevens.com. For a free color catalog of all our high-quality books, call toll free 1-800-542-2595 or fax 1-877-542-2596.

Library of Congress Cataloging-in-Publication Data

Fittleworth, George, author.
 Your stomach / George Fittleworth.
     pages cm. — (Know your body)
 Includes bibliographical references and index.
ISBN 978-1-4824-4458-2 (pbk.)
ISBN 978-1-4824-4402-5 (6 pack)
ISBN 978-1-4824-4422-3 (library binding)
1. Stomach—Juvenile literature. 2. Digestive organs—Juvenile literature. 3. Human physiology—Juvenile literature. I. Title.
 QP151.F55 2017
 612.3'2—dc23
                                    2015021480

Published in 2017 by
Gareth Stevens Publishing
111 East 14th Street, Suite 349
New York, NY 10003

Copyright © 2017 Gareth Stevens Publishing

Designer: Andrea Davison-Bartolotta
Editor: Therese Shea

Photo credits: Cover, p. 1 Catherine Delahaye/Getty Images; pp. 3, 4, 6, 8, 10, 12, 14, 16, 18, 20, 22–24 Anna Frajtova/Shutterstock.com; p. 5 S K Chavan/Shutterstock.com; p. 7 Blend Images - Ronnie Kaufman/Larry Hirshowitz/Getty Images; p. 9 dr OX/Shutterstock.com; p. 11 Creatas Images/Creatas/Thinkstock; p. 13 (main) Kraig Scarbinsky/DigitalVision/Thinkstock; p. 13 (inset) Dorling Kindersley/Getty Images; p. 15 (main) Stockbyte/Thinkstock; p. 15 (inset) Designua/Shutterstock.com; p. 17 (main) Natalia Mylove/Shutterstock.com; p. 17 (inset) Mehmet Cetin/Shutterstock.com; p. 19 Sebastian Kaulitzki/Shutterstock.com; p. 21 monkeybusinessimages/iStock/Thinkstock.

All rights reserved. No part of this book may be reproduced in any form without permission in writing from the publisher, except by a reviewer.

Printed in the United States of America

CPSIA compliance information: Batch #CS16GS: For further information contact Gareth Stevens, New York, New York at 1-800-542-2595.

CONTENTS

Boldface words appear in the glossary.

Your Super Stomach

Your stomach is an **organ** that's shaped like the letter J. It's found in the upper left side of your belly. The stomach has several jobs. It stores food. It breaks it down for the body's use. It also kills **germs** in food.

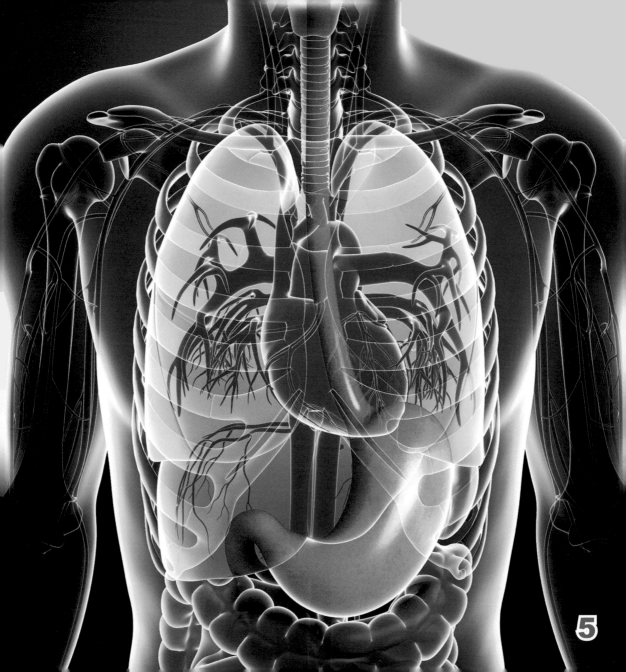

The stomach of an adult is about 10 inches (25 cm) long. However, it can **stretch** a lot! When your stomach is empty, it has folds in its sides. The folds disappear as the stomach fills with food and liquid.

Your Digestive System

The digestive system is made up of many body parts that work together to turn food into forms that the body can use. Your stomach is just one organ in your digestive system. However, it's a very important organ!

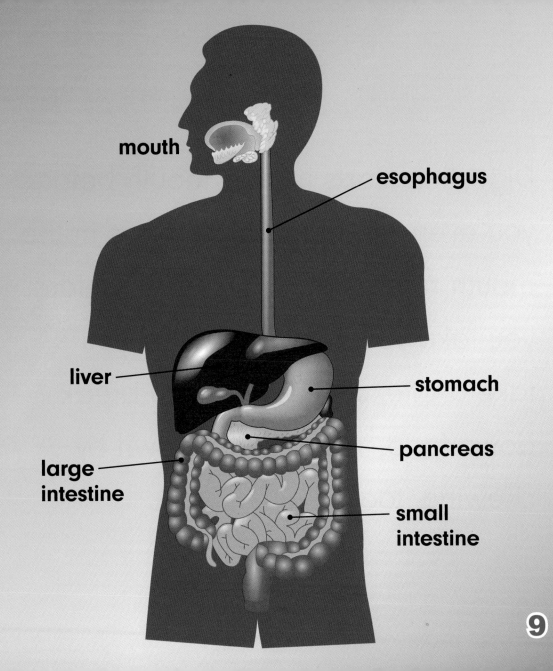

mouth

esophagus

liver

stomach

pancreas

large
intestine

small
intestine

9

Digestion starts in your mouth before you even begin to eat! **Glands** in the mouth **release** saliva, or spit, before you take your first bite. Once you take a bite, saliva begins to break down food. You break it down by chewing, too.

When you swallow, the food goes into a tube called the esophagus (ih-SAH-fah-guhs). **Muscles** move to push the food down the esophagus into the stomach in just a few seconds. You swallow air, too. That's why you burp!

Glands in the stomach release digestive juices. These strong liquids break down food even more and kill germs. The juices could harm the stomach, so the stomach is lined with **mucus**. Stomach muscles mix the food and juices.

Some foods such as meats and beans may stay in the stomach for 5 hours. However, sugars travel through the stomach in as quickly as 1 hour and don't make us feel as full. The stomach moves all food to the small intestine next.

sugars

meat

beans

In the small intestine, juices from the liver and pancreas break down food more. The food's **nutrients** are taken into the body. What's left over travels into the large intestine. The last nutrients are removed, and the solid waste is pushed out.

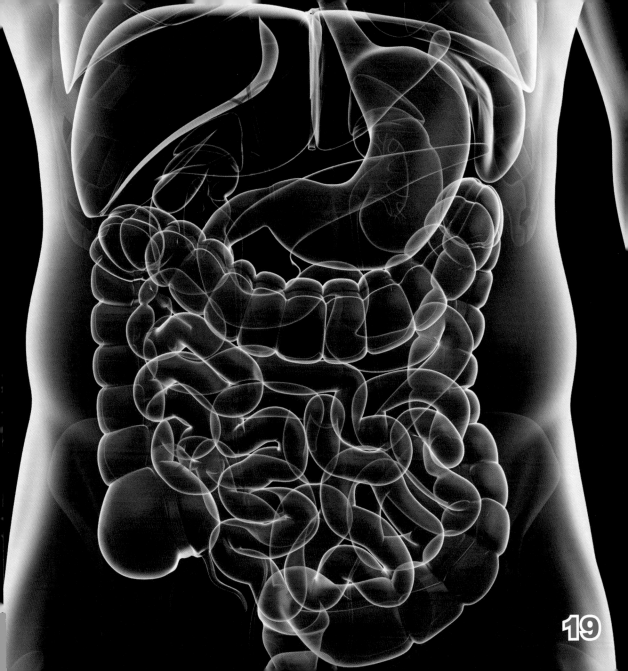

19

What's That Sound?

Even when your stomach's empty, the muscles still move. That's why your stomach makes sounds when you're hungry. Make sure you eat healthy foods to give your stomach and the rest of your body parts the many nutrients they need!

GLOSSARY

germ: a tiny living thing that can cause illness

gland: a body part that produces something needed for a bodily function

mucus: a thick slime produced by the bodies of many animals

muscle: one of the parts of the body that allow movement

nutrient: something a living thing needs to grow and stay alive

organ: a part inside a body that has a job to do

release: to let out

stretch: to lengthen or widen

FOR MORE INFORMATION

BOOKS

Bailey, Jacqui. *What Happens When You Eat?* New York, NY: PowerKids Press, 2009.

Burstein, John. *The Dynamic Digestive System: How Does My Stomach Work?* New York, NY: Crabtree Publishing, 2009.

Cobb, Vicki. *Your Body Battles a Stomachache.* Minneapolis, MN: Millbrook Press, 2009.

WEBSITES

The Stomach Facts
www.softschools.com/facts/human_body/the_stomach_facts/341/
Find out some cool facts about your stomach.

Your Digestive System
kidshealth.org/kid/htbw/digestive_system.html
Read more about your super stomach and digestive system.

Publisher's note to educators and parents: Our editors have carefully reviewed these websites to ensure that they are suitable for students. Many websites change frequently, however, and we cannot guarantee that a site's future contents will continue to meet our high standards of quality and educational value. Be advised that students should be closely supervised whenever they access the Internet.

INDEX